Written and Illustrated by Caroline Arnold

A Day and Night on the
PRAIRIE

PICTURE WINDOW BOOKS
a capstone imprint

Wee-o! Wee-o! call the prairie dogs.

It is a cool spring morning on the prairie. One by one the prairie dogs pop out of their holes and look for fresh grass to eat. If they see a predator, they will dash back into their burrows.

Prairie dogs live in groups called towns. Some towns are home to hundreds of prairie dogs.

The pronghorn antelope are hungry too.
They snip off leaves and flowers with sharp
front teeth. If any pronghorn senses danger,
it will raise the hairs on its rump and alert
the rest of the herd. Then all the animals
will race across the prairie to safety.

A male meadowlark sings. His mate snaps up spiders and insects with her long bill. She will take them back to her nest to feed her hungry chicks.

In a sunny spot nearby, a box turtle warms itself. Soon it will search for insects, worms, and berries to eat. If a large animal comes near, the box turtle will pull its head, tail, and legs into its hard shell. Even the sharp teeth of a fox or coyote cannot bite through it.

Box turtle shells are hinged on the bottom. They allow the turtles to pull in all their soft body parts and protect them from predators.

The day grows warmer. A hawk spreads its wings to catch a rising air current. It soars over the prairie, looking for rabbits, prairie dogs, and other small animals to eat. When the hawk spots its prey, it dives and grabs the prey with its sharp talons.

A bison herd moves across the prairie. Young bison stay close to their mothers. The bison bite off clumps of grass. They chew slowly, grinding the plants with their large back teeth.

Bison are the largest animals on the prairie. Females may weigh more than 1,000 pounds (454 kilograms). Males are often twice as heavy! A newborn bison calf weighs about 65 pounds (29 kg).

3:00 P.M.

All day long an orb-weaving spider sits in her web. She waits for a fly, bee, or grasshopper to get stuck in the silky threads. Once her prey is caught, the spider wraps it to eat later.

Nearby a garter snake slips through the grass. It flicks its forked tongue while hunting for toads, worms, and other small animals. It follows their smell. If the sun becomes too hot, the garter snake will look for a shady spot to stay cool.

Snakes that live on the prairie include garter snakes, king snakes, ringneck snakes, and rattlesnakes.

By early evening the prairie dogs have gone back into their burrows. Most birds have found roosts for the night. A jackrabbit nibbles leaves before settling down to rest under a bush.

In the fading light, a burrowing owl leaves its underground home. It perches on a mound of dirt. When the owl hears a vole running through the grass, it swoops down on silent wings. It snatches the vole with its talons. The owl will hunt again at dawn.

An empty prairie dog burrow makes a good place for a burrowing owl to build its nest.

Ribbit! Ribbit! Frogs croak at the edge of a small pond. Bats swoop over the dark water and catch moths and mosquitoes. A family of skunks stops for a drink.

A thirsty fox waits until the skunks have gone before coming to the pond. It does not want to get sprayed by them. After drinking, the fox hunts for mice and small animals. It may eat berries and seeds too.

Whoo! Whoo! calls an owl. It searches on silent wings for rats, mice, and other small animals. It catches them with its sharp talons. The owl carries its prey back to its nest.

A rattlesnake injects venom into its prey through hollow, pointed teeth called fangs.

13

MIDNIGHT

The cool midnight air is full of life. Bats swoop in the dark sky. Some chase tiny insects. Others drink nectar from cactus flowers.

A water hole in the desert is called an oasis.

A-roo! A-roo! howls a coyote. All night long it hunts for food. It will eat insects, lizards, mice, fruit, or whatever it can find. When the coyote finds a water hole, it stops for a drink. Scorpions and tarantulas crawl nearby, looking for spiders and insects to eat.

All through the night, desert animals are busy looking for food. A kangaroo rat finds some seeds and stuffs them into pouches in its cheeks. It will store the seeds in its burrow.

A kangaroo rat has long hind legs.
It can leap several feet in one hop.

A kit fox looks and listens for rats and mice. Its large ears can hear their tiny, high-pitched sounds. The kit fox sees a kangaroo rat and pounces. But just in time, the kangaroo rat leaps away to safety.

The sky grows light, and the sun peeks over the horizon. Nighttime animals settle down for the day. Owls return to their nests, the kit fox goes to its burrow, and the peccaries curl up for a nap. It is time for daytime animals to wake up and start a new day. Lizards warm themselves, jackrabbits find leaves to nibble, and birds collect food for their young.

Every day and every night, animals find food, water, and safe places to rest in the desert. It provides them with everything they need.

What Is a Desert?

A desert is a dry place. It gets less than 10 inches (25 centimeters) of rain a year. There are four major deserts in North America: the Great Basin, the Mojave [muh-HAHV-ee], the Chihuahuan [chee-WA-wan], and the Sonoran.

The Sonoran Desert covers parts of Arizona, California, and the Mexican states of Baja California and Sonora. In summer, daytime temperatures can reach higher than 110 degrees Fahrenheit (43 degrees Celsius). In winter, nighttime temperatures can drop below freezing. Plants and animals that live in the Sonoran Desert are adapted to its extreme climate.

Throughout the day and night, animals are busy in the desert. Diurnal animals are active during the day. Nocturnal animals are active at night. Which animals in this book are diurnal? Which are nocturnal? Where do they live in the desert?

Where Can You Find Deserts?

Deserts are found all around the world. Some are hot. Others are cold. The largest desert in the world is the Sahara Desert, in Africa. It covers more than 3 million square miles (7.8 million square kilometers). Only about one-fifth of the world's deserts are sandy. Most deserts, including those in the United States, are rocky or mountainous.

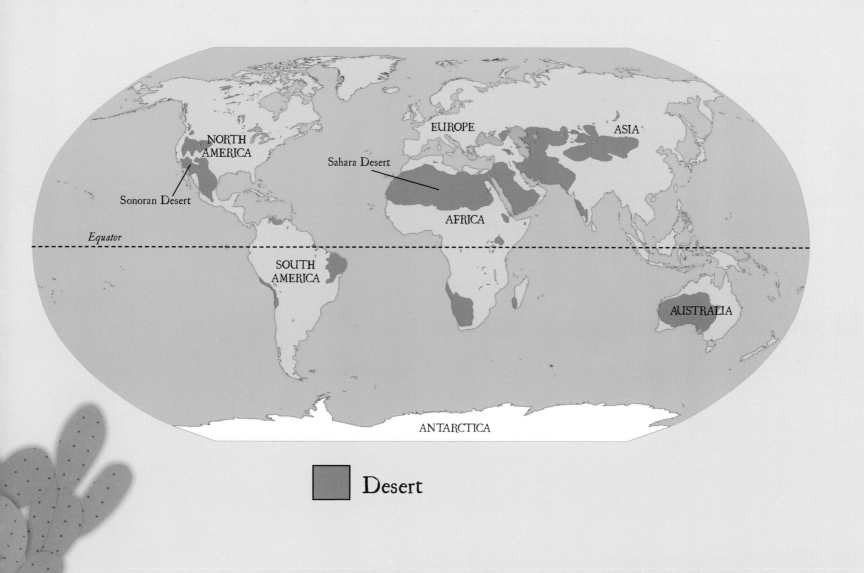

NORTH AMERICA

Sonoran Desert

EUROPE

ASIA

Sahara Desert

AFRICA

Equator

SOUTH AMERICA

AUSTRALIA

ANTARCTICA

Desert

Fun Facts

- A jackrabbit's large ears help it stay cool. Blood flowing through the ears allows extra body heat to pass into the outside air.

- The Gila monster is the only venomous lizard in the United States. Its bright colors warn predators to stay away.

- Thick coats protect bighorn sheep from the hot desert sun during the day. They keep the sheep warm at night.

- Desert tortoises dig shallow holes in the ground. When it rains the holes fill with water for the tortoises to drink.

- A roadrunner doesn't usually fly, but it is a speedy runner. It can run up to 20 miles (32 kilometers) per hour as it chases prey.

- When peccaries sense danger, they cough loudly and produce a smelly odor. To defend themselves from predators, they use their knife-like tusks.

- Scorpions often bury themselves in sand to avoid the hot sun. The scorpion's hard outer shell helps keep moisture inside its body.

- Stiff tufts of hair protect the bottoms of a kit fox's feet from the hot desert ground.

Critical Thinking Using the Common Core

1. Describe how the passing of time is shown throughout this book. (Integration of Knowledge and Ideas)

2. Name three diurnal predators in the Sonoran Desert and their prey. Then name three nocturnal predators and their prey. (Key Ideas and Details)

Glossary

adapt—to change to fit into a new or different environment

burrow—a tunnel or hole in the ground made or used by an animal for shelter

cactus pad—the flat, paddle-shaped stem of certain cacti, such as the prickly pear

climate—average weather of a place throughout the year

diurnal—active during the day

habitat—the natural home or environment of an animal, plant, or other living thing

horizon—the line where the sky and the earth or sea seem to meet

inject—to put into

nectar—a sweet liquid found in many flowers

nocturnal—active at night

predator—an animal that hunts other animals for food

prey—an animal hunted by another animal for food

talon—a long, sharp claw of a bird

venomous—full of venom, a poison injected into a victim by biting or stinging

vibrate—to move back and forth quickly

Read More

Anderson, Sheila. *What Can Live in a Desert?* Animal Adaptations. Minneapolis: Lerner Publications, 2011.

Pattison, Darcy. *Desert Baths.* Mt. Pleasant, S.C.: Sylvan Dell Pub., 2012.

Rissman, Rebecca. *Living and Nonliving in the Desert.* Is It Living or Nonliving? Chicago: Capstone Raintree, 2014.

Slade, Suzanne. *What Eats What in a Desert Food Chain?* Food Chains. North Mankato, Minn.: Picture Window Books, 2013.

Index

Internet Sites

FactHound offers a safe, fun way to find Internet sites related to this book. All of the sites on FactHound have been researched by our staff.

Here's all you do:

Visit *www.facthound.com*

Type in this code: 9781479560721

Super-cool stuff! Check out projects, games and lots more at www.capstonekids.com

Thanks to our advisers for their expertise, research, and advice:

Cecil R. Schwalbe, PhD, Wildlife and Fisheries Program
University of Arizona, Tucson

Terry Flaherty, PhD, Professor of English
Minnesota State University, Mankato

Editor: Jill Kalz
Designer: Lori Bye
Art Director: Nathan Gassman
Production Specialist: Kathy McColley
The illustrations in this book were created with cut paper.
Design Elements: Shutterstock/Alfondo de Tomas (map),
    Alvaro Cabrera Jimenez

Picture Window Books are published by Capstone,
1710 Roe Crest Drive, North Mankato, Minnesota 56003
www.capstonepub.com

Library of Congress Cataloging-in-Publication Data
Arnold, Caroline, author, illustrator.
 A day and night in the desert / written and illustrated by Caroline Arnold.
    pages cm.—(Nonfiction picture books. Caroline Arnold's habitats)
 Summary: "Highlights the activities of animals in the Sonoran Desert during one average 24-hour period"—Provided by publisher.
 Audience: K to grade 3.
 Includes bibliographical references and index.
 ISBN 978-1-4795-6072-1 (library binding)
 ISBN 978-1-4795-6084-4 (paperback)
 ISBN 978-1-4795-6144-5 (eBook PDF)
1. Desert animals—Behavior—Juvenile literature. 2. Desert animals—Juvenile literature. 3. Sonoran Desert—Juvenile literature. I. Title
 QL116.A74 2015
 591.754 2 23   2014025333

Look for all the books in the series:

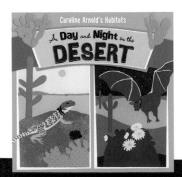

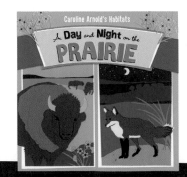

Printed in the United States of America in North Mankato, Minnesota   092014   008482CGS15